Halloween

Costumes and Treats on All Hallows' Eve

Fay Robinson

E **Enslow Publishers, Inc.**

40 Industrial Road PO Box 38
Box 398 Aldershot
Berkeley Heights, NJ 07922 Hants GU12 6BP
USA UK

http://www.enslow.com

Library of Congress Cataloging-in-Publication Data

Robinson, Fay.
Halloween—Costumes and treats on All Hallows' Eve / Fay Robinson.
      p. cm. – (Finding out about holidays)
Includes bibliographical references and index.
ISBN 0-7660-1632-3
1. Halloween—Juvenile literature. I. Title. II. Series.
GT4965 .R63   2001
394.2646—dc21
      00-010909

Printed in the United States of America

10 9 8 7 6 5 4 3 2 1

To Our Readers:
All Internet Addresses in this book were active and appropriate when we went to press.
Any comments or suggestions can be sent by e-mail to Comments@enslow.com or to the
address on the back cover.

Photo Credits: Archive Photos, pp. 14, 18, 20, 22, 26, 34, 37, 38, 41, 42, 48; Corel Corporation, pp. 2, 4, 6, 10 (both), 11, 12, 13 (top), 17, 29, 39; Courtesy of Nina Rosenstein, pp. 31, 32; Hemera Technologies Inc., 1997–2000, pp. 1, 3, 7 (both), 9, 13 (bottom), 15, 16 (both), 21, 23 (both), 25, 27 (top), 30, 33, 35, 36 (both), 44 (all), 45 (all); Hulton Getty Collection/Archive Photos, pp. 24, 27 (bottom), 28, 40, 46; Lambert/Archive Photos, pp. 5, 47; Popperfoto/Archive Photos, pp. 8, 19.

Cover Photo: Courtesy of Nina Rosenstein (background); © Corel Corporation (all insets).

CONTENTS

★

A Halloween celebration would not be complete without pumpkins, costumes, and treats.

CHAPTER 1

Trick or Treat!

It is a crisp October evening in the northeastern part of the United States. Red and yellow leaves blow around on the ground. Other leaves on tree branches move back and forth in the wind.

Children put on costumes. They cover their faces with makeup. Some friends arrive. They are all dressed in different costumes. They each have a bag for collecting treats.

They run to a neighbor's house. White threads like cobwebs dangle from the trees. A jack-o'-lantern with a glowing face seems to be watching. Scary music is coming from inside the house.

Halloween would not be complete without treats of all shapes and sizes.

One of the children rings the doorbell and the door slowly opens. The person behind it is ready. "Trick or treat!" everyone shouts. The neighbor smiles and pushes a bowl full of candy toward the group. Each person takes a piece and drops it into their bag. What could be more fun?

It is Halloween. It is a time to dress up, be scared in a fun way, and get treats. But where did these customs come from? Why do we wear costumes? Who decided we should be scared in a fun way? And why do we say trick or treat?

Getting candy and treats is all part of the fun on Halloween.

The story of this holiday goes back many, many years. As a matter of fact, Halloween is one of our oldest holidays. Just how did it get started?

This boy and girl check out a glowing Halloween jack-o-lantern.

CHAPTER 2

Halloween's Beginnings

AUTUMN TIME

★

In some parts of the country, the weather gets colder, and leaves turn colors and begin to fall off of the trees in October. It was this change in the seasons that may have led to some of the traditions on Halloween.

As October comes to an end, the days get shorter and the nights get longer. In some parts of the country, the weather turns cool and crisp as winter approaches. It can be an exciting time. Some children look forward to playing in the snow and spending time with their family.

But long, long ago, things were different. There were no electric lights. So most activities had to stop when the sun went down. There was no indoor heat. People bundled up and stayed by fires to keep warm. As the leaves fell from trees

Long ago, the Celts believed in a sun god. They had a special day to thank and honor him. Stonehenge in England (bottom) was a place for religious ceremonies related to the rising and setting of the sun.

and plants died, people were frightened. To some, winter seemed like a time of death.

More than two thousand years ago, a group of people called the Celts (Kelts) lived in Great Britain and Ireland. To explain the things they did not understand, the Celts believed in many gods. Some of the gods were good and some were evil. The sun god was good. The sun gives light and heat. Why did the sun seem to go away as winter came? Would the sun's light come back? The Celts were not sure. To thank the sun god, they had a day to honor him. This day was the last day of their year—October 31.

This celebration of the sun was mixed with fears about winter. Some stories tell of an evil god who came on this same day. This god, named Samhain (Sow-in), was the god of death. People believed he invited the ghosts of the dead to join him. People did not know what the ghosts might do. People thought the ghosts might enter their bodies or the bodies of animals. They thought the ghosts might even pick out who would die in the next year.

The Celts were afraid that the sun would not return when winter came.

Because Halloween started so long ago, we cannot be sure what people did or believed then. We must count on the stories people told over time. Some stories say Samhain was a god who caused a lot of trouble on October 31.

Long ago, some people believed that the god of death invited the ghosts of the dead to join him.

Other stories say there never was a god named Samhain. The word *Samhain* simply means "end of summer." Some stories say ghosts came to earth on their own. People were afraid of these ghosts. They built huge outdoor fires to scare the ghosts away. People wore costumes made of animal skins to frighten the ghosts. They left food outside their homes, hoping the ghosts would enjoy the food instead of coming inside.

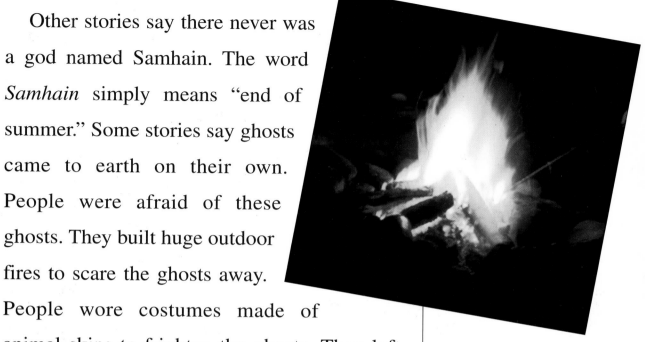

Some stories say that people built huge outdoor fires to scare ghosts away.

The Celts named this event Samhain, after the god who frightened them. It was the beginning of winter, and the beginning of Halloween. But there is more to learn about Halloween than that.

A young girl dressed as a witch pulls a message out of a carved pumpkin. Jack-o'-lanterns light up behind her.

CHAPTER 3

A Brew of Holidays

Samhain is the earliest event that led to today's Halloween. But it is not the only one. Three other holidays also added their customs.

In about the year A.D. 43, a group of people called the Romans took over lands owned by the Celts. The Romans, like the Celts, believed in many gods. One was Pomona, a beautiful maiden. She was the goddess of fruit and orchards. She wore a crown of apples on her head and carried fruit in her arms. Near November 1, the Romans celebrated Pomona and the harvest

Long ago, people gave away gifts of fruits and nuts to celebrate Pomona, the Roman goddess of fruit.

with a festival. People gave away gifts of fruits and nuts. They played games and ran races.

About six hundred years later, the Roman Catholic Church created All Saints' Day. This holiday honored all their saints. It was first celebrated in the spring. The Church later changed the date to November 1, the day after Samhain. The Church did not like Samhain, because it was about evil. The Church wanted to replace Samhain with a religious holiday. They called it All Hallows, which meant "all saints." The night before was called All Hallows' Evening. This was soon shortened to Hallows' Eve, then Halloween.

Around A.D. 1000, the Church made another holiday called All Souls' Day. This holiday was celebrated on November 2. On this day the souls of people who had died were remembered. In England on this day, the poor went door-to-door. They sang and begged for food at each home. Families would give out money or special cakes called soul cakes. In return, the poor promised to pray for the family members who had died. This activity was called going a-souling.

The idea of going door-to-door to get Halloween treats came from the old activity of going a-souling.

A young boy and girl bob for apples at a Halloween party. A large jack-o-lantern lights up the background.

These holiday traditions have blended together to create our modern Halloween. From Samhain, we get costumes and the idea of a spooky night. From Pomona, we get food and games, such as bobbing for apples. From All Saints' Day we get the name Halloween. From All Souls' Day, we get going door-to-door for treats.

BLESSING A SNEEZE

Some people believed that when they sneezed, their souls were blown out of their bodies. If the devil was quick enough, they thought he could take their souls. People started saying "God bless you" to keep this from happening. Today, people still say "God bless you" when someone sneezes. But few people believe their souls will be stolen by the devil.

A long time ago, some people believed that when they sneezed, their souls were blown out of their bodies. People began to say "God bless you" as a way to stop this from happening.

19

Witches on broomsticks are a well-known part of Halloween. But, how did we get the idea that witches could fly?

CHAPTER 4

Spooky Things

Where did we get ideas about witches flying on broomsticks, skeletons, tombstones, and jack-o'-lanterns as symbols of Halloween?

JACK-O'-LANTERNS

One story of Halloween is about jack-o'-lanterns. Jack was a very bad man, the story goes. When he died, he could not get into heaven. Even the devil did not want him in hell. So Jack was forced to walk about the earth without a resting place. When Jack complained

When people from other places began to arrive in the United States from Europe in about the year 1500, most of them had not yet started to celebrate Halloween. Halloween did not become a popular holiday in America until around the 1840s when large numbers of Irish people arrived. The Irish brought many of their customs to the United States, including Halloween.

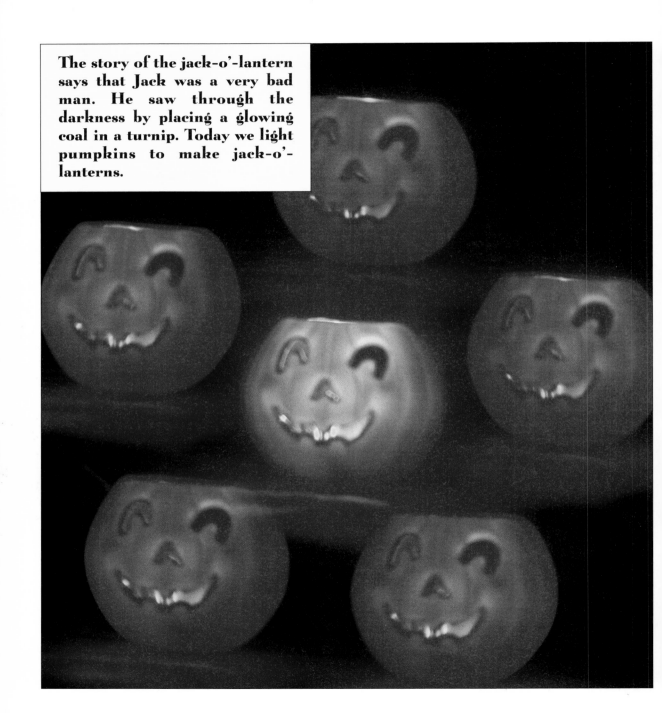

The story of the jack-o'-lantern says that Jack was a very bad man. He saw through the darkness by placing a glowing coal in a turnip. Today we light pumpkins to make jack-o'-lanterns.

that he could not see in the dark, the devil threw a glowing coal to him. Jack placed the coal in a turnip he had been eating. He used the turnip as a lantern. The story says that poor Jack is still wandering the earth today.

The Irish put coals inside turnips on Halloween, just like Jack in the story. They carved scary faces on turnips. When the Irish came to America, they used pumpkins instead, which were easier to carve than turnips.

Now we do the same thing. It is fun to carve a funny or scary face in a pumpkin. With a flashlight inside, the pumpkin glows just like a lantern.

Ghosts, goblins, and ghouls are all part of the holiday fun.

GHOSTS, SKELETONS, AND TOMBSTONES

The Celts believed ghosts wandered the earth on Halloween. They also thought that ghosts

The Celts of long ago believed that skeletons danced in graveyards on Halloween night.

and skeletons danced in graveyards on that night. They believed that skeletons rattled their bones as they danced.

Ghosts and skeletons are favorite decorations on Halloween today. People also put make-believe tombstones in their yards to make them look like graveyards.

WEARING COSTUMES

On the night of Samhain, the Celts of long ago wore scary costumes. They wanted to frighten away the ghosts whom they believed were around. Or, some people say, they wore spooky costumes so the ghosts would think they were already dead. That way, the ghosts would pick on someone else. Now all the real fear is gone from

Long ago, people wore scary costumes to frighten away ghosts. Today, we wear scary costumes just for fun.

Dressing up for Halloween is lots of fun!

Halloween. We wear scary costumes just for the fun of it.

W I T C H E S

Long ago, people worried a lot about witches. Witches were thought to be ugly and evil. People believed they had magic powers. They could cast spells to cause terrible storms. They could make people sick or turn them into toads. People thought the witches could turn themselves into animals. That way, people never knew if a witch was nearby. People blamed witches for any bad thing they could not explain.

One of the times that witches got together was on Halloween. On that

Witches were thought to be ugly and evil. Some people believed that witches had magical powers.

27

night, it is said that witches would fly through the sky on broomsticks. They would dance and chant around a bonfire.

Today there are still people who call themselves witches. They are not ugly or bad. They just have their own beliefs.

BLACK CATS

Many people believed black cats were witches' pets. Some people even thought witches could turn themselves into black cats. Then the cats had the powers of witches. Because people were so afraid of witches, they were afraid of black cats, too.

TRICK-OR-TREATING

How did the custom trick-or-treating begin? One explanation comes from Samhain. To

Some people believed that witches could turn themselves into black cats. Then, the cats would have the power of witches.

Trick-or-treating may have started as a way to keep the ghosts happy.

keep the ghosts from harming them on this night, the Celts put out treats to keep the ghosts happy. When the poor ate the food, people believed the ghosts had eaten it. If no food was left out, the poor might play a trick. Then people would blame it on the ghosts.

Another story from the Celts tells about a god named Muck Olla. It was said that Muck Olla brought luck and wealth. On Samhain a man wearing a horse costume led the poor from house to house. They told each family to give them gifts for Muck Olla. If the family did not, Muck Olla would bring them bad luck. Most families gave food to the group, such as potatoes, milk, or eggs. If they did not, the poor would play a trick.

Trick-or-treating may also have started

Some Celts believed that Muck Olla would bring them good luck if they gave gifts to the poor.

Going door-to-door for candy and treats on Halloween became popular in America in the 1840s.

Costume parades at
school may also be a
part of Halloween.

with going a-souling on All Souls' Day. That was when the poor would go door-to-door, begging for food and offering to pray for the souls of the dead.

No matter how it started, going door-to-door for treats became popular in America in the 1840s.

The phrase *trick or treat* means "give me a treat or I'll play a trick!" But people were going trick-or-treating for one hundred years before they started using those words. It was not until the1940s that the phrase trick or treat was used.

The phrase "trick or treat" was first used in the 1940s.

Witches, skeletons, graveyards, and black cats are all very scary things. But, on Halloween people can be scared in a fun way.

CHAPTER 5

Happy Halloween!

Black cats, ghosts, skeletons, and graveyards—they are all very scary things. But on Halloween, trick-or-treaters can be scared in a harmless way. Wearing costumes and putting up scary decorations is just pretend.

SAFETY FIRST

People do not need to be afraid of black cats, ghosts, and skeletons on Halloween, but they should still be careful when they go trick-or-treating. Here are some Halloween safety tips:

SCARY BUT FUN

Halloween might have started out as a scary holiday. But today, we can be scared in a fun, harmless way. Trick-or-treating and going to parties are fun things to do to celebrate Halloween.

All across America, people dress up and celebrate in fun ways on Halloween.

✔ Wear reflective tape on costumes. That way cars can see you in the dark.

✔ Make sure masks allow clear vision. Makeup is also a good choice.

✔ Put a flashlights inside jack-o'-lanterns, not candles.

✔ Stay on well-lit streets. Cross only at corners.

✔ Young children should always go trick-or-treating with an adult.

✔ Have an adult at home check treats before eating them.

All across America, people dress up and do scary things on Halloween. They celebrate in just about the same way everywhere. The only differences are in the kind of parties schools or towns have or whether or not trick-or-treating is done. Lots of children like to wear scary

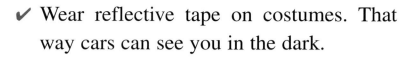

People do not need to be scared on Halloween. But, trick-or-treaters do need to be careful when they go out.

costumes, like the Celts of long ago. Many children dress up as ghosts, jack-o'-lanterns, skeletons, witches, or even black cats. There are other scary costumes, too, such as spiders, bats, vampires, and Frankenstein monsters.

But costumes do not have to be scary. Funny or pretty costumes are good also. Some people dress as ballet dancers, bees, butterflies, and characters from books. Costumes can be handmade or store-bought. It is fun to pretend to be someone or something else for one night.

Some schools or towns have Halloween parades. Children get to show off their costumes in front of a crowd. After the parade is over, they might get special treats.

Some towns have pumpkin contests. The biggest or best decorated pumpkin might win.

Halloween parties with scary music and plastic bats can be a fun way to celebrate with friends.

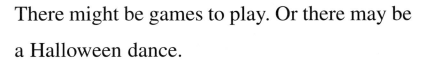

There might be games to play. Or there may be a Halloween dance.

Some towns have pumpkin contests. The biggest pumpkin wins. Other towns have scarecrow festivals. People put out scarecrows they make for everyone to see. There might be apple cider, hot cocoa, and different foods made from apples or pumpkins, such as breads, pies, and other treats.

In many places, children go trick-or-treating. The people who answer the door may be wearing a costume too. They might be playing scary music. But even if they are not in costume, they will have treats.

Some children stay home part of the time to answer the door. Then they can scare visitors by playing creepy music and dressing in a costume. People usually give away candy for treats. But coins, party favors, small plastic bats, or plastic spiders may also be given.

Sometimes people have Halloween parties. Here are some ideas to make a great Halloween party.

Turn the lights down low. The dark can make things seem scarier. Make a tape recording of weird sounds, such as moans, screams, and howls. Rattle sticks to sound like skeleton bones. Play creepy music.

Decorate the party room with spooky things such as jack-o'-lanterns, tombstones, and skeletons. Use lots of black and orange—they are the colors of Halloween.

Plan to play some games, such as bobbing

This woman, dressed as a nurse, shakes hands with a life-sized skeleton.

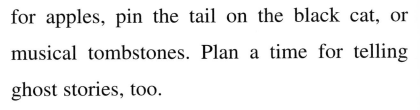

Wearing costumes, like this witch's mask, is just one of the many things that Americans do when Halloween arrives.

for apples, pin the tail on the black cat, or musical tombstones. Plan a time for telling ghost stories, too.

Make a hall of horrors. First, put out some "monster parts." Peeled grapes can feel like eyeballs. Gelatin with fruit in it can feel like a monster's guts. A bowl of cooked noodles can feel like brains. Then, lead kids through the dark, touching the "monster parts" as they go.

Whether trick-or-treating, going to a parade, or having a party, Halloween is all about having a good time.

HALLOWEEN SHOPPING

Americans spend more than $2 billion each Halloween. Christmas is the only holiday on which more is spent.

Halloween Craft Project

★

Mini Ghosts

Get into that Halloween spirit. Here you will make some ghoulish ghosts to decorate and greet trick or treaters. You will need:

✔ **several pieces of white tissue paper**

✔ **several small rubber bands**

✔ **a black marker**

✔ **string or fishing line**

1. Take one piece of tissue paper and crumple it into a ball.

2. Lay a second piece of tissue paper flat on a table. Place the balled-up tissue in the center of the flat piece of tissue paper.

3. Pull the flat tissue around the ball and bunch it together. Put a rubber band around the bottom of it. This is the head and neck of the mini ghost.

4. Draw eyes and a mouth on your ghost with the black marker.

5. Tie a piece of string or fishing line to the rubber band. (Hint: If it is tied to the back of the ghost's head, the ghost will look like it is flying.)

*Safety Note: Be sure to ask for help from an adult, if needed, to complete this project.

6. Make several ghosts. Tie them to tree branches in your yard or string them around your doorway.

Words to Know

★

All Saints' Day—A holiday that honors the saints of the Catholic Church.

All Souls' Day—A holiday that honors people who have died.

celebration—A way of observing a holiday or an event.

Celts—A group of people who lived in Great Britain and Ireland more than two thousand years ago and the people who are related to them today.

custom—The way a group of people does something.

decorations—Things people put around their home or office to make it look special.

Words to Know

★

goddess—A female god.

jack-o'-lantern—A carved out pumpkin that is lit up.

Pomona—The Roman goddess of fruits and orchards.

saint—Someone who is officially recognized by the Church for holiness.

Samhain—The god of death and the holiday that marked the end of summer for the Celts of long ago.

trick-or-treating—Dressing in costume and going door-to-door for treats on Halloween.

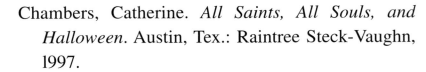

Reading About

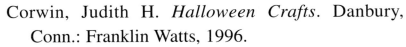

Chambers, Catherine. *All Saints, All Souls, and Halloween*. Austin, Tex.: Raintree Steck-Vaughn, 1997.

Corwin, Judith H. *Halloween Crafts*. Danbury, Conn.: Franklin Watts, 1996.

Hintz, Martin, and Katie Hintz. *Halloween*. Minneapolis, Minn.: Capstone Press, 1996.

Leiner, Katherine. *Halloween*. New York: Simon & Schuster Children's Books, 1993.

Stamper, Judith B. *Halloween Fun Activity Book*. Mahway, N.J.: Troll Communications, 1997.

Internet Addresses

★

CLEMSON UNIVERSITY'S COOPERATIVE
EXTENSION SERVICE HALLOWEEN
SAFETY PAGE
<http://virtual.clemson.edu/groups/FieldOps/
     Cgs/hallow2.htm>

HALLOWEEN FUN FOR KIDS
<http://www.bestweb.net/~wallnut/halloween/
     index.html>

KID'S DOMAIN HALLOWEEN GAMES
<http://www.kidsdomain.com/games/hall.html>

SAFESURF'S HALLOWEEN FUN PAGE
<http://www.safesurf.com/halloween/>

Index

s:\comm\jobs\...\duecard1.qxd 10/00

BAKER & TAYLOR